MW01148328

THE CAFÉ BRÛLOT

THE CAFÉ BRÛLOT

SUE STRACHAN

LOUISIANA STATE UNIVERSITY PRESS

BATON ROUGE

Published by Louisiana State University Press
www.lsupress.org

Manufactured in the United States of America
First printing

Designers: Michelle A. Neustrom and Barbara Neely Bourgoyne
Typeface: Arno Pro
Printer and binder: Integrated Book International (IBI)

Portions of the section "At Broussard's" appeared in *Preservation in Print,* March 2020.

Frontispiece, Introduction, and Resources photos by Chris Granger (chrisgranger.com).
Photo on page 54 courtesy of Antoine's Restaurant.

Library of Congress Cataloging-in-Publication Data

Names: Strachan, Sue, author.
Title: The café brûlot / Sue Strachan.
Description: Baton Rouge : Louisiana State University Press, 2021. |
   Includes bibliographical references.
Identifiers: LCCN 2021004097 | ISBN 978-0-8071-7604-7 (cloth)
Subjects: LCSH: Cooking, American—Louisiana style. | LCGFT: Cookbooks.
Classification: LCC TX715.2.L68 S 2021 | DDC 641.59763—dc23
LC record available at https://lccn.loc.gov/2021004097

To the bartenders, waiters, and restaurants of New Orleans,

carrying the torch for the city's cocktails and other drinks

CONTENTS

ACKNOWLEDGMENTS

Writing about the history of a beloved New Orleans drink was a bit intimidating. There are so many great resources—I feared overlooking someone with important details to add, and for that, I apologize. But as most culinary historians can tell you, there is always more to discover. Thank you, Louisiana State University Press editor Jenny Keegan, who enlisted me for this project, for your patience, and to the rest of the LSU Press staff.

The staff of the Museum of the American Cocktail, part of the Southern Food & Beverage Museum, was so generous with their time and resources, particularly in the museum's John and Bonnie Boyd Hospitality and Culinary Library. Many thanks to founder Elizabeth M. Williams, who steered me in all sorts of amazing directions; executive director Brent Rosen; and Gracie Goodrich. Williams is also an author of multiple books about drinks and food. Check them out.

More knowledge came from Ned Hemard, a historian whose research is an essential resource when doing any book about New Orleans history. Poppy Tooker, author, radio host, TV personality, culinary historian, and chef, was another amazing resource. Wayne Curtis also helped with my trail for Armagnac and the possible origins of Café Brûlot, as did John DeMers. Both Curtis and DeMers are expert authors in their respective libation and culinary realms. Another expert is David Wondrich, barroom historian and writer, whose knowledge is nonpareil.

When the Armagnac trail grew cold, a friend, Andrew Nelson, suggested I contact Kimberly Noelle Charles of Charles Communications Associates, which specializes in promoting wine, microbreweries, specialty and organic spirits, and other beverages and food. She immediately reached out to her sources, including Odila Galer-Noel of PRonCall, who put me in touch with May Matta-Aliah, the U.S. educator for Armagnac, who in turn, forwarded me to Amanda Garnham, attachée de presse for the Bureau

National Interprofessionel de l'Armagnac, who provided me with the answers I needed. This all happened within less than forty-eight hours! Thank you for the connections and information.

I couldn't have done this book without the help of Antoine's owners, Lisa and Rick Blount (by the way, Lisa is a fantastic food and drink stylist); Arnaud's co-owner Katy Casbarian; Brennan's co-owner Ralph Brennan; media relations guru Simone Rathle of SimoneInk; Broussard's owners, Marv, Richy, and Zeid Ammari, and general manager Rebecca Schattman; Commander's Palace's Lally Brennan and Ti Martin; and Galatoire's general manager Melvin Rodrigue, who also let me taste the difference between curaçao, triple sec, and Grand Marnier.

More appreciation to Charles Carter, a longtime waiter at Antoine's; Augie Spicuzza, the maître d' at Arnaud's; Charles Abbyad, semiretired waiter and maître d' of Arnaud's; and Neal Bodenheimer, co-owner of Cure and Cane & Table, for their patience with the multitude of questions I asked. By coincidence, it is Neal's father, Henry Bodenheimer, who helped Allstate Sugar Bowl director of communications and media relations John Sudsbury identify a few of the who's who in the Sugar Bowl photos from Antoine's.

Always a great resource is Kevin Williams, of the Southeastern Architectural Archives at Tulane University, who directed me to his coworkers at the university's Special Collections at Howard-Tilton Library, for the historic Sugar Bowl menu. Kerry Moody, at Decorations Lucullus, showed me around the company's design and antiques studio, which was a treat.

If you are a writer—neophyte or experienced—I recommend joining the Authors Guild, a group that provides a wealth of information and support. I loved working with Guild executive director Isabel Howe.

I spent a lovely afternoon sampling coffees with Kevin Pedeaux of Coast Roast Coffee and Tea. I dislike coffee—Café Brûlot is one of the only coffee-based drinks I will consume—but it was a great education, and you might just see me having a cup of coffee and chicory soon.

Thanks to the photographers Josh Brasted and Chris Granger, who are talented and fun to work with. I recommend them both. Check out their websites at joshbrasted.com and chrisgranger.com. And last but certainly not least, thank you to D, W, and L—because you always have to acknowledge your feline supporters.

THE CAFÉ BRÛLOT

INTRODUCTION

No one ever forgets his or her first Café Brûlot.

It's the alluring scent that seduces: a combination of cloves, citrus, cinnamon, and maybe a slight hint of brandy. For me it smells like Christmas, a time of year that is sometimes overlooked for its olfactory pleasures.

Next up is the visual panache, as the waiter finally arrives at your table with a gueridon—tableside service—to do the presentation. Depending on the restaurant, even on the waiter, the demonstration could include an orange peel studded with cloves dangling above the bowl that is then

doused with flaming alcohol. The coffee is added slowly, finishing the blaze of glory.

But the process isn't yet complete: The brew is poured into special brûlot cups and saucers—adorned with a roguish devil.

So much drama and flair befits Café Brûlot, a drink that could have only been invented—or depending on your preferred history, perfected—in New Orleans, where a sumptuous meal doesn't feel complete without it.

Translated as "incendiary coffee," some also call it Café Brûlot Diabolique, "devilishly incendiary coffee." Some ingredients change depending on what restaurant makes it, but the base ingredients are coffee, brandy, sugar, cinnamon, lemon, oranges, cloves, and usually an orange liqueur. Ordinary ingredients, but how they are put together is what make this drink extraordinary.

It's a favorite at the old-line restaurants in New Orleans such as Arnaud's, Brennan's, Broussard's, Commander's

Opposite: Arnaud's Charles Abbyad pours the Café Brûlot mixture, which is on fire, down the orange peel studded with cloves, then ladles the finished product into a brûlot cup. *Photos by Josh Brasted.*

Palace, Galatoire's, and Antoine's, where Jules Alciatore whipped up the first batch in the United States in the 1880s.

Or perhaps it was pirate Jean Lafitte back in the early nineteenth century?

Or is it a centuries-old drink from the Armagnac region of France, made to celebrate post distillation of Armagnac (brandy), that migrated to New Orleans?

It was not invented during Prohibition in the United States, to mask the smell of alcohol, as some books suggest.

The origins of Café Brûlot can be a little murky, as many culinary and cocktail tales may be, but still very entertaining.

CHAPTER ONE

THE DEVIL MADE ME DO IT

THE ORIGINS OF CAFÉ BRÛLOT

> There can't be good living where there are not good drinks.
>
> —BENJAMIN FRANKLIN

Many believe New Orleans is where the cocktail was invented—that in the 1830s, apothecary Antoine Peychaud (of Peychaud's bitters fame) served a mixed brandy drink in an egg cup, called a *coquetier* in French, the word *cocktail* evolving from that.

5

Alas, great story, not quite true. There was an actual Mr. Peychaud who lived in New Orleans, but that's not the who, when, and where of how cocktails were invented.

There is, of course, more than one theory—here are two, for example, in no particular order. During America's Colonial period, tavern keepers would combine the remains—the tailings—from the casks into one, serving it from a spigot, which was referred to as the "cock." Soon patrons were asking for the less expensive drink, "cock tailings." Another—proposed by barroom and alcohol historian David Wondrich—is a little less savory: In the eighteenth century, horse traders would place ginger in a horse's ass to perk up—cock—its tail, making it frisky. It also turns out that tavern owners would add the same spices to invigorate a drink, an eye-opener in the morning.

What is a cocktail? A modern-day definition, courtesy of the *Merriam-Webster Dictionary,* is "a usually iced drink of wine or distilled liquor mixed with flavoring ingredients." Some cocktail historians hark back to an earlier definition that says a cocktail originally referred to a specific blend of alcohol, sugar, water, and bitters and was sometimes called a "bittered sling."

Whatever the origin or definition of *cocktail,* it would be hard to dispute that New Orleanians perfected these libations.

Cocktails invented in New Orleans include the Sazerac, Brandy Crusta, Brandy Milk Punch, Absinthe Frappé, Ramos Gin Fizz, Roffignac, Grasshopper, Vieux Carré, and Hurricane. While some histories give years or decades for their creation, research can also produce a mix of results.

Can Café Brûlot be added to that list? Depends on what definition of *cocktail* you want to believe as well as when the spark was first lit.

So let's get started on this journey, part time travel, part culinary coincidence.

THE LEGEND

It had probably been a good run on Barataria Bay for Jean Lafitte (also spelled Laffite), pirate, businessman, and

JEAN LAFITTE

Jean Lafitte is a celebrated and controversial character in New Orleans lore. Details of his early life are often murky—some say he was born in France and arrived in New Orleans in the early nineteenth century; other sources state he was born in the French colony of Saint-Domingue (now Haiti) around 1780, arriving in New Orleans with his mother and older brother, Pierre, who spent time as a privateer before becoming a blacksmith. They were rumored to have a warehouse on Royal Street, while New Orleans legend says it is on Bourbon Street, where Lafitte's Blacksmith Shop Bar is now. This building on Bourbon Street is one of the oldest in the city, constructed between 1722 and 1732 by Nicolas Touze, and houses one of the oldest bars in the United States.

It was Barataria Bay's strategic importance as an approach to New Orleans and Lafitte's knowledge of the area that attracted the British during the War of 1812 (1812–15). Lafitte and his crew were offered British citizenship and land grants in the British colonies in America if they assisted in the naval fight against the United States. Lafitte was also asked to return whatever he had taken from Spanish ships—Spain and Great Britain were allies. A refusal would mean the destruction of Barataria.

Lafitte pondered his choices, believing the Americans would win. However, before he committed to helping the United States, there was a little matter of his brother, Pierre Lafitte, who was in an American prison. After some assurances, Pierre Lafitte conveniently "broke" out of prison. Unfortunately, the Americans still didn't trust Jean Lafitte and attacked his ships. Governor William C. C. Claiborne, who swung between trying to jail Lafitte and lauding him, eventually recommended him to Gen. Andrew Jackson. It took some convincing, even after they were promised pardons, for Lafitte and his men to aid the Americans. But they did and helped defeat the British in the Battle of New Orleans on January 8, 1815.

But you can't keep a privateer from being a privateer—and Lafitte continued his career from his new base in Galveston, Texas, then in Cuba. Supposedly, he was buried at sea in the Gulf of Honduras.

Of course, that isn't the end of the story.

Lafitte allegedly buried treasure in a number of locations, including Galveston and coastal Louisiana, where Lake Charles has an annual Pirate Festival, formerly called "Contraband Days." Rumor has it that Lafitte's favorite hideout was Contraband Bayou in Lake Charles and that it is where he buried his gold treasure. Grand Isle, a barrier island in southeastern Louisiana, is rumored to have been a hiding spot as well.

His name also lives on: in addition to Lafitte's Blacksmith Shop Bar, there is also Jean Lafitte National Historical Park and Preserve and a town named Jean Lafitte in southeastern Louisiana.

Jean Lafitte was also the inspiration for books. Many believe that Lord Byron's poem *The Corsair* (1814) was written about Lafitte, as was *Lafitte the Pirate* (1930) by Lyle Saxon. It was this book that Cecil B. DeMille used for the movie *The Buccaneer* (1938), starring Fredric March as Lafitte, cinematically illustrating Lafitte's contributions to the War of 1812. The film was remade in 1958, with Yul Brynner as Lafitte and Charlton Heston as Andrew Jackson.

New Orleans citizen. Most likely it was nighttime, and some corners of the Vieux Carré (French Quarter) were still awake, and that's where Lafitte and his crew were celebrating their latest foray.

The Louisiana Purchase in 1803 had made New Orleans a newly minted U.S. territory, and even though Americans had started to settle in the city, it was still dominated by a mélange of Creoles, enslaved people, free people of color, Native Americans, and Spanish and French, those two countries having bounced New Orleans back and forth for almost one hundred years. Businessmen of legal and illegal means flocked to the city, which was the focus of trade across the entire Mississippi River valley.

Lafitte was part of that crew, and while he was known as a smuggler and a privateer, his brother Pierre Lafitte, a blacksmith, also kept their more legal businesses going in New Orleans. His blacksmith shop allegedly served as a repository for smuggled goods, including enslaved people, into the city.

Lafitte, not one to shy away from a drink, and in honor of his good fortune, had Café Brûlot made.

Maybe.

Lafitte had another partner in pirating, Dominique You, who some say was the first Café Brûlot fan.

But were they drinking Café Brûlot, or was it just Brûlot?

LA FLAMME DE L'ARMAGNAC

For this, we travel to the Armagnac region in France, where Brûlot has been made for centuries. It is produced in the Armagnac region in Gascony and is considered the oldest brandy distilled in France.

"Brûlot is indeed an Armagnac tradition," said Amanda Garnham, attachée de presse for the Bureau National Interprofessionel de l'Armagnac.

"The Brûlot in Armagnac is made during the distillation period, called 'La Flamme de l'Armagnac,'" said Garnham. This period runs from mid-October generally to the end of January, with the legal cutoff point for Armagnac distillation on March 31 of the year following the harvest.

"During 'La Flamme de l'Armagnac,' the Armagnac producers open their doors to visitors, clients, friends, for typical Gascon lunches and dinners next to the copper alembic as new eau-de-vie flows, and it is normally at the end of these feasts that the Brûlot is served after the coffee," said Garnham.

Brûlot is the newly distilled eau-de-vie (brandy) taken off the alembic, a distilling apparatus, at full degrees of alcohol. Garnham noted that in Armagnac, the producers distill around 52–62 percent alcohol by volume (abv) in general, depending on the grape variety (legal limits are 52 to 72.4 percent abv), then it is put into a big copper cauldron or basin, and sugar is added.

"Each producer seems to have its own 'secret recipe,'" she said. "Some add nothing other than sugar, whereas others add dried fruits, citrus fruits, cloves, then it is lit. . . . The flaming bowl is stirred continuously with a long handled copper bowled ladle and the blue flames rise high as some of the alcohol disappears."

Guests, who are there to celebrate the distillation, then stoke the flames for a while.

Garnham added, "Brûlot is warm, sweetly perfumed, and 'prescribed' to ward off any colds or flu during the winter months."

BACK TO THE LEGEND

So, what about early-nineteenth-century privateers Jean Lafitte and Dominique You? Was the fiery drink they were imbibing the same Brûlot? It's a good possibility. Lafitte is thought to have been born in either the French Basque country, in southwestern France, or Saint-Domingue, present-day Haiti; You was originally from Sète, in the Languedoc region in the South of France.

Armagnac is in southwestern France, so if Lafitte was from France, he might have sampled Brûlot or seen it made. Although You was from a region east of Armagnac, there is a chance the drink migrated in that direction and that he was familiar with it too.

Then there is Lafcadio Hearn's *La Cuisine Créole,* a New Orleans cookbook published in 1885, which mentions

CAFÉ DIABLO
OR CAFÉ DIABLE

Take out brandy and replace it with rum, and what do you have? Café Diablo.

Rum instead of brandy, why not? And with New Orleans's Spanish heritage—it was a Spanish territory from 1762 to 1801—it could have also been a drink consumed by Jean Lafitte and Dominique You.

There are a number of recipes on the internet that mirror Café Brûlot but are called "Café Diablo" and, in some cases, "Café Diable." In *Gourmet's Guide to New Orleans: Creole Cookbook,* first published in 1933, in addition to recipes for Café Brûlot, there is one for Café Diable, which adds apple peels, coffee beans, and nutmeg to the same basic ingredients as Café Brûlot.

One restaurant in Miami hedged its bets. A 1954 menu from the Saxony Hotel's Veranda Room restaurant included both Café Diablo and Café Brûlot.

Brûlot but calls it "Grand Brulé à la Boulanger": "The crowning of a grand dinner is a brulé. It is the pièce de résistance, the grandest pousse café of all."

But unlike today's Café Brûlot, the recipe didn't use orange liqueur but kirsch (also known as Kirschwasser, a cherry liqueur). Nor did it have coffee; the *brulé* was French brandy, kirsh, cinnamon, allspice, and sugar. Hearn recommended dimming the lights before lighting it on fire. The Petit Brulé in the book is made with an orange, with the hollowed-out orange creating a "cup," in which it is served; it was also served with no coffee.

Was it Jules Alciatore of Antoine's Restaurant in New Orleans who added the coffee?

According to *Phillip Collier's Mixing New Orleans*, Alciatore was "inspired by French bon vivants who would drown a sugar cube in Cognac and place it over an open flame before extinguishing it in a cup of hot coffee." This goes along with one of the definitions of *Brûlot:* "Coffee served with alcohol or certain spices." (*Brûlot* also means: fire ship; scathing report; or in Quebec, an insect of the family Ceratopogonidae, the no-see-um).

But where does that leave the Armagnac Brûlot and the recipes from Hearn's cookbook from 1885? Both could have served as an inspiration for what Jules Alciatore created: Café Brûlot Diabolique.

JULES ALCIATORE AND CAFÉ BRÛLOT

It was the 1880s in New Orleans, and Jules Alciatore had taken over the family business, Antoine's, not long after his father's death in 1877. The restaurant's menu of French cuisine enhanced with local and Spanish influences made it popular with natives and out-of-town visitors. Alciatore was also an innovator, often creating new menu items or changing recipes to keep his customers intrigued.

Oysters Rockefeller, for example, was invented by Jules Alciatore in 1899, when there was a shortage of snails coming from Europe to the United States. Using oysters in their place was his solution, and as they were local, he wasn't tied to the tides of trade—only nature. Alciatore then created a sauce with greens—the recipe is still a secret—that when combined created such a richness that he named it after John D. Rockefeller, one of the wealthiest men in the United States at that time. Another original oyster dish by Alciatore was oysters Foch, named after World War I marshal Ferdinand Foch, for whom the restaurant and the Knights of Columbus hosted an honorary breakfast.

Alciatore adapted the recipe for Pompano Montgolfier that his father, Antoine Alciatore, had created, turning it into Pompano en Papillote. It was created for a banquet honoring Brazilian balloonist Alberto Santos-Dumont. The dish is a pompano in a sauce of wine, shrimp, and crabmeat that is baked in a sealed parchment paper envelope, which should puff up with steam, like a balloon.

And there's more: eggs Sardou is a dish named for Victorien Sardou, a famous French dramatist of the nineteenth century, who was a guest in New Orleans when the dish was invented. The ingredients have gone through a slight change over time: when presented to Mr. Sardou, it was poached eggs with artichoke hearts, ham, anchovies, truffles, and hollandaise sauce. Today it is a little different, with poached eggs, creamed spinach, and hollandaise sauce on artichoke bottoms and can vary from restaurant to restaurant.

Antoine Alciatore, the founder of Antoine's in 1840, brought *pommes de terre soufflés*—better known as puffed, or soufflé, potatoes—to the United States. It turns out Alciatore was in the right place at the right time, working in the kitchen of Chef Jean-Louis Françoise-Collinet, who also invented béarnaise sauce. The potatoes were concocted in 1837, a result of a king running late. It was the inaugural run of the new train line from Paris to St. Germain-en-Laye for King Louis Philippe of France, and a delay of the king's arrival forced Chef Collinet to reheat half-cooked potatoes that were pulled from the hot grease. The half-cooked potatoes puffed up, and the future Antoine's Restaurant signature dish was born.

When he was of age, Jules Alciatore was sent to France to apprentice with chefs, so there is a possibility he encountered the Armagnac Brûlot and no doubt enjoyed many a coffee drink, with and without alcohol enhancing it. But was a version of Café Brûlot already in New Orleans, via the French who had moved to the city, possibly sipped by Jean Lafitte and Dominique You? And dousing the flames with coffee, a popular drink, doesn't seem out of the realm of possibilities. (The popularity of coffee can be attributed to Pope Clement VIII, whose papacy lasted from 1592 to 1605. The Catholic Church wanted to ban it, but when he tasted coffee, he said, "The devil's drink is so delicious we should cheat the devil by baptizing it!" And coffee spread throughout Europe.)

Some point in the 1880s is when Jules Alciatore is thought to have created Café Brûlot Diabolique, making it "devilishly burnt coffee" by adding the *diabolique,* Why? Probably a good marketing tool, adding a tinge of "danger." Alciatore designed the unique brûlot cups—based on the demitasse—and saucers adorned with devils as well as the brûlot bowl and stand, its legs in the shape of a devil. These are still used at Antoine's today.

It is thought that the dapper devil was inspired by the character of Mephistopheles in Johann Wolfgang von Goethe's *Faust,* published in 1808, with part 2 following in 1832. The tragic play was based on the German legend originating in the late fifteenth and early sixteenth centuries about a man, Johann Georg Faust (ca. 1480–1540), who in real life was an alchemist and practiced necromancy but, according to chapbooks (small books) of that time, was dealing with the devil. It is men's clothing from the period, the German Renaissance, that can be seen interpreted on the brûlot cups, saucers, and stand: a schaube (a type of coat only higher-class men could wear), which could be interpreted artistically as a jacket with a cape; stockings with trousers; and a hat, sometimes including feathers. As it turns out, this German Renaissance devil was also popular in nineteenth-century advertisements and art. So, it is not hard to imagine where Jules Alciatore got his idea for adorning the accoutrements and the flaming drink.

And there may be an interesting predecessor to Café Brûlot Diabolique: an Antoine's menu from 1881 has Café Cognac on it. Was this a name change or a completely different drink?

Café Brûlot spread, for lack of a better way of saying it, like fire. An 1896 ad from Waldhorn Company, an antique store, included a recipe for making Café Brûlot with cinnamon, cloves, lemon peel, brandy, sugar, and French coffee.

And let's not forget other New Orleans restaurant proprietors who were born in the southwest of France, who probably sampled Brûlot growing up and helped popularize the American version: Jean Galatoire, the founder of Galatoire's, left Pardies, France, in 1874, and Count Arnaud Cazenave, who founded Arnaud's, was born in Bosdarros, France, in 1876.

Other old-line New Orleans restaurants began serving the brew, including Broussard's (founded 1920), Brennan's (founded 1955), and Commander's Palace (founded 1893, with the part of the Brennan family taking over in 1969).

As the nineteenth century turned into the twentieth, the drink's popularity endured. An interesting note is that Café Brûlot did not appear on the Antoine's menu from 1910 to 1940, though Orange Brûlot, like Hearn's recipe, remained. Was Café Brûlot an off-menu item that those in the know could order? A bit of this time period coincides with Prohibition (1920–33), and there are cocktail and history books that claim Café Brûlot was invented then to cover the smell of alcohol. (How did they explain the source of the flame because you needed alcohol for that!)

CAFÉ BRÛLOT FAN CLUB

In 1937, post-Prohibition, President Franklin D. Roosevelt had lunch at Antoine's Restaurant with city leaders. The menu included oysters Rockefeller, Pompano en Papillote, Baked Alaska, and Café Brûlot. It was at this lunch, during the appetizer, that New Orleans mayor Robert Maestri famously commented to Roosevelt, in his New Orleans accent, "How you like dem erstas?" about the city's famed oysters.

In a souvenir booklet that Antoine's produced for the restaurant's hundredth anniversary, in 1940, Café Brûlot Diabolique got rave reviews: "Upon tasting the Café Brûlot Diabolique, Bob Davis, roving correspondent of the *New York Sun,* exclaimed, 'I, the Imperial ambassador from the immeasurable pit, pronounce your Café Brûlot Diabolique and quintessence of Hell's best, brewed in the pit where all incomparable sinners take their vow and declare that death hath no sting and the grave no victory."

Other raves came from John Ringling of circus fame,

President Roosevelt's lunch with city leaders at Antoine's in 1937. Seated in foreground at left: President Roosevelt's son Elliott, Louisiana governor Richard Leche, the president, New Orleans mayor Robert Maestri. Standing and leaning toward the president is Louisiana WPA director James. M. Crutcher. Behind Crutcher in the bow tie is Antoine's proprietor, Roy Alciatore. *Photo by E. S. Martin. Courtesy of Louisiana Division/ City Archives, New Orleans Public Library.*

A souvenir book from Antoine's Restaurant recommends Café Brûlot Diabolique and Orange Brûlot. *Photo by Chris Granger.*

who said, "What could be more sublime than to taste the delights of heaven while beholding the terrors of Hell?"

Dorothy Dix, of the *Picayune* newspaper in New Orleans, called it "liquid fruitcake," and short story writer O. Henry was a fan. A Tulane University humor journal, *Café Brulo* (how they spelled it), was revived "after a quarter of a century," then banned after two issues in 1922 because of jokes, not mentioned in the *New Orleans Item* article about it, that offended students and faculty, particularly those at Newcomb College, the women's college affiliated with Tulane University.

Café Brûlot also inspired a soft drink. For a short time in the early twentieth century, Hotel Grunwald Caterers made soda called "Café-NOLA (Brulo)," proclaiming in an ad to be "the Spicy Drink," the bottle adorned with a devil that looks much like the one on the side of the brûlot cups designed by Jules Alciatore. It tasted like Café Brûlot but without the alcohol, allegedly.

In the mid-twentieth century, newspapers recounted the popularity of the drink being served at ladies' luncheons and at home. While some accounts said the popularity waned after the turn of the century, for New Orleans families, the tradition endured. Carla Morphy Adams said it was always served on "Thanksgiving and Christmas" at home, with her parents "allowing us to drink it as kids." She even received a brûlot setup as a wedding gift, when she married Jay Adams.

And while the old-line restaurants served the drink, in 1975, the restaurant Café Brûlot opened at 322 Magazine Street, in the city's former coffee district. Owned by Blaise and Margaret D'Antoni, the restaurant served Creole and Italian food. The location now has another restaurant.

Café Brûlot's origin story takes a few twist and turns, but that hasn't really affected its popularity or fiery, celebratory reputation.

Menu

❦

Celeri et Olives

Huitres Bourguignonne

Filet de truite Amandine

Pommes de Terre Souflées

Tournedos de boeuf marchand de vin

Salad Antoine

Biscuit Glacée

Petit Fours

Café Brulot Diabolique

APERITIFS

VINS
BLANC MAISON
ROUGE MAISON

THE SUGAR BOWL AND
CAFÉ BRÛLOT

What says U.S. college football more than two coaches "making" Café Brûlot before a big game?

During the mid-twentieth century, it was a Sugar Bowl tradition for the competing football coaches to make—or in their case, stir, then pose for a photo—Café Brûlot at Antoine's the night before the big game. Legendary football coaches such as Bear Bryant (University of Alabama and University of Kentucky), Paul Dietzel (Louisiana State University Tigers), and Johnny Vaught (University of Mississippi) all stirred the incendiary brew.

Opposite: Antoine's traditionally hosted dinner on the night before the Sugar Bowl, and the opposing coaches would "make" Café Brûlot. This menu is for the 1968 Sugar Bowl, when the University of Wyoming played against Louisiana State University. The coaches were Charles McClendon for LSU and Lloyd Eaton for Wyoming. LSU won 20 to 13. *Photo courtesy of Louisiana Menu and Restaurant Collection, Louisiana Research Collection, Tulane University Special Collections, Howard-Tilton Memorial Library.*

Sugar Bowl dinner at Antoine's in 1964. Johnny Vaught, coach of the Ole Miss Rebels, and Paul "Bear" Bryant, coach of the University of Alabama Crimson Tide, stir Café Brûlot. Alabama won 12 to 7. *Photo by Leon Trice. Courtesy of Louisiana Division/City Archives, New Orleans Public Library.*

CHAPTER TWO

Speak of the Devil

INGREDIENTS

Simplicity is the ultimate sophistication.

—LEONARDO DA VINCI

The composition of Café Brûlot is not complicated: coffee; brandy or cognac; an orange liqueur, such as curaçao, triple sec, Grand Marnier, or Cointreau; sugar; cloves; cinnamon; oranges and lemons.

As with any great cocktail, using the freshest of ingredients makes an important difference in the final product. Another bonus? Some have medicinal qualities. Cheers!

COFFEE

Let's start with coffee. Antoine's waiter Charles Carter recommends French roast instead of coffee with chicory. But over at Arnaud's, coffee with chicory is used, so it really is a taste preference. To me, the coffee with chicory in Arnaud's Café Brûlot gives a spicy kick to it.

If you don't drink coffee or don't know the difference between coffees, head over to your local coffee shop to see if they have some brewed to taste. Much like comparing wines, you can tell the differences between blends more easily when sampling several at one time.

ORANGES AND LEMONS

Use only fresh oranges and lemons. The oranges should have a thin, smooth skin and no soft spots; and the lemons must have a bright yellow rind and zesty aroma.

COFFEE, CHICORY, AND NEW ORLEANS

Coffee and chicory is often assumed to be a uniquely New Orleans blend. Alas, while the city has a love for it, its origins started overseas.

Chicory is a blue-flowered perennial, its name probably derived from the Egyptian word *Ctchorium*. The plant was cultivated in Egypt at least five thousand years ago, where it was used mainly for animal feed and medicinal purposes, as it was believed to be good for the liver.

Its root, after it is roasted and ground, is added to coffee.

The Dutch were the first to mix coffee and chicory, around the late eighteenth century. The blend was introduced to France in 1801 by M. Orban of Liège (then France, now Belgium) and M. Giraud of Horning (actually Hornaing, near Valenciennes, France), according to the nineteenth-century writer Peter Simmonds in *Coffee and Chicory: Their Culture, Chemical Composition, Preparation for Market and Consumption*.

Some sources say that chicory in coffee started appearing in New Orleans during the American Civil War after Union blockades cut off the city's port, starting in April 1862. New Orleanians, still needing a coffee fix, looked for ways to stretch out the supply, which, in addition to chicory, included acorns and beets.

But remember New Orleans's French roots? Chicory had already been mixed with coffee in France, becoming popular in the nineteenth century, after the Continental Blockade that Napoleon Bonaparte initiated in 1808, depriving France of most of its coffee. Even after the blockade, the French continued to use chicory, believing it was good for health and improved the flavor of coffee.

So, when the Civil War arrived in New Orleans, its citizens were more than likely already drinking coffee flavored with chicory.

Today chicory for coffee is grown in France and South Africa as well as Nebraska in the United States.

Fun fact: When you drink chicory and coffee, you won't get an added buzz because chicory does not have caffeine in it.

CLOVES

Cloves should be aromatic and whole, not ground, when making Café Brûlot. Whole cloves, if stored in an airtight container, should last a year.

Cloves are the dried, unopened flower buds of the clove tree, a tropical evergreen known as *Syzygium aromaticum*. It is native to Indonesia but can also be found in India, Pakistan, Sri Lanka, the Comoros, Madagascar, the Seychelles, and Tanzania. The spice adds flavor to dishes and is thought to have potential health benefits, such as supporting liver health and helping stabilize blood sugar levels.

CINNAMON

Cinnamon sticks are made out of the inner layer of bark from several trees species from the genus *Cinnamomum*. After extracting it from the outer bark, the inner bark is dried, naturally curling into rolls, which are also called "quills."

Cinnamon mainly comes from Indonesia but also from China, Vietnam, and Sri Lanka. Like cloves, it has potential health benefits such as reducing inflammation and providing antioxidants.

SUGAR

Use white granulated sugar for Café Brûlot.

LIQUOR AND LIQUEURS

Last, but certainly not least, are the liquor and liqueurs. The key is that they have enough alcohol content—80 proof and above—to produce a steady flame.

Brandy refers to a distilled spirit made from fermented fruit juice, using grapes or other fruit. It can be made anywhere. Cognac, called "liquor of the gods" by French author Victor Hugo, is a brandy, with a few crucial differences. It can only be produced in the Cognac region, in

Arnaud's Charles Abbyad pours sugar into Café Brûlot. *Photo by Josh Brasted.*

southwestern France, and must be made from white grapes from one of six different *terroirs*. The liquid must be distilled twice, with the season running between October 1 and March 31.

Armagnac is made in southwestern France in the province of Armagnac in Gascony. It's good to note that Jean Galatoire, who established Galatoire's Restaurant, and the founder of Arnaud's, Count Arnaud Cazenave, came from this region, so it's easy to assume they both sampled Brûlot.

Curaçao, triple sec, and Grand Marnier are orange liqueurs that are often interchangeable in a recipe, though each will impart a different flavor. Some people like Cointreau.

But let's start at the beginning of what can be a somewhat confusing exploration of the differences between all of them.

The journey of curaçao, the liqueur, started in the Caribbean, when in 1527 the Spanish landed on Curaçao, an island off the coast of Venezuela. Among the items they brought were Valencia oranges, which they planted. However, after harvesting the oranges, they realized the island's dry climate produced a bitter fruit.

By the 1600s, the Dutch had arrived, discovering wild orange groves. The bitter oranges were called "Laraha," and at some point—no one knows when—someone figured out that these orange peels, when dried in the sun, contained etheric oils with an enchanting fragrance. The dried peels were brought back to the Netherlands, where the Bols company was already making a number of flavored liqueurs.

Then, about two hundred years later, the French came along and invented triple sec—the origin of its name still debated. The *triple* is thought to refer to triple distillation, while some believe it is because three types of oranges are used. *Sec* is "dry" in French.

The general differences between curaçao and triple sec is that curaçao is usually pot distilled with brandy, cognac, or sugarcane alcohol, and triple sec is column distilled with a neutral grain alcohol and is drier.

Cointreau is an orange-flavored triple sec liqueur produced in Saint-Barthélemy-d'Anjou, France. The distillery was founded in 1849 by Adolphe Cointreau. The liqueur is blended with sweet and bitter orange peels and pure alcohol from sugar beets, with the first bottles sold in 1875.

Grand Marnier's roots go back to France, when in 1880

Louis-Alexandre Marnier Lapostolle combined cognac and a bitter orange from the Caribbean. Marnier first called it "Curaçao Marnier," but the name was changed when César Ritz, founder of the Hôtel Ritz Paris, came up with "Grand Marnier," calling it "A Grand Name for a 'Grand Liqueur!'"

It is usually more expensive, and of the three orange liqueurs, Grand Marnier can be sipped on its own, just like Cointreau, which some people prefer. Curaçao and triple sec may seem too sweet to sip and are better mixed into other cocktails.

But do you really need the orange liqueur? Elizabeth M. Williams, founder of the Southern Food & Beverage Museum, said that there is no need for orange liqueur because the mixture is already getting citrus flavoring from the heated or flamed lemon and orange peels.

"The oils in the lemon and orange peels that get flamed and put into the mixture will give you the same flavor," said Williams.

KIRSCHWASSER EAU-DE-VIE INSTEAD OF ORANGE LIQUEUR

When looking at videos on how to make Café Brûlot, I came across one by Dale DeGroff, "King of Cocktails," in which he used Kirschwasser instead of an orange liqueur. Kirshwasser is a clear brandy in which the flavor of cherries comes through but is not overpowering. When I told Antoine's Lisa Blount about that, she agreed that it could have been used instead of orange liqueur in Café Brûlot's early years, as now in DeGroff's recipe.

It was also mentioned as an ingredient in Lafcadio Hearn's *La Cuisine Créole,* published in 1885, for the Grand Brulé à la Boulanger. Referred to as "kirsch, the same of maraschino," it seems to replace the orange liqueur. The recipe features almost all of the same ingredients minus the coffee and orange liqueur, though Hearn does say, "Green tea and champagne are sometimes added." If you decide to make Café Brûlot with Kirschwasser, remember it is more flammable than the orange liqueurs. It also gives the Café Brûlot a smoother and more of what I call a "schnapps" taste than if you use an orange liqueur or no liqueur.

CHAPTER THREE

The Devil Is in the Details

THE RIGHT EQUIPMENT FOR CAFÉ BRÛLOT

He who is best prepared can best serve his moment of inspiration.

— SAMUEL TAYLOR COLERIDGE

Café Brûlot is unique in the drink and cocktail realm because the equipment used to make it and to serve it is specifically designed for the potent brew. The most identifiable are the brûlot cups and saucers. We can thank Antoine's Jules Alciatore for that.

The brûlot cup that Jules Alciatore designed. *Photo by Chris Granger.*

While there is no definitive date when Alciatore designed the cups and saucers, the red-caped devil adorning both is much more mischievous than scary. Elizabeth M. Williams at the Southern Food & Beverage Museum in New Orleans says the devil used on the cups and saucers is inspired by the character of Mephistopheles in Johann Wolfgang von Goethe's *Faust,* the first part published in 1808, with part 2 following in 1832. The tragic play was based on the German legend of the late fifteenth and early sixteenth centuries about an alchemist, Johann Georg Faust (ca. 1480–1540), who practiced necromancy but was thought to be serving the devil.

This German Renaissance devil was also popular in nineteenth-century advertisements and art. Artist Eugène Delacroix's print *Mephistopheles and His Drinking Companions* (1828) resembles the image on the cups and saucers, as does Antoine "Tony" Johannot's illustration of Mephistopheles thought to have been completed between 1845 and 1847.

Williams thinks that the look is based on what a German nobleman might have worn at that time, noting the sword and the feather in the cap. Men's clothing from the period included a *schaube*, stockings with trousers, and a hat, which sometimes held a feather. The image endures, and if you check out devilish art from the Belle Epoque (1871–1914), the figure has a similar look.

It was also a clever way to market the drink because Antoine's Restaurant called it Café Brûlot Diabolique—the *diabolique* adding the devilish inference.

Finding antique sets of cups and saucers can be hard, but it is worth checking out New Orleans's antiques stores. The online store eBay is also a good resource for antique and new sets, and Cocktail Kingdom sells new ones on its website. However, if you don't have the devilish cup and saucers, demitasses are a good alternative.

Kerry Moody at Decorations Lucullus in New Orleans often finds what he calls Café Brûlot cups on his buying trips in France, but these are not in the Alciatore design. They are demitasses made with a thicker glass. When a

Opposite: Faust and Mephisto in Faust's Study, 1845–47, engraving by Tony Johannot, after *Faust,* by Johann Wolfgang von Goethe.

person has finished the coffee drink, they can flip it over; there is an indentation in the bottom of the cup in which a shot of calvados, or the digestif of choice, can be poured, then imbibed, noted Moody.

Brûlot bowls can be silver-plated, stainless steel, or copper lined with silver. Rick Blount, fifth-generation owner of Antoine's, prefers silver over stainless steel because of the lush, whoosh sound the ladle makes against the silver, unlike the clanking of stainless steel. There is also the conductive issue: silver is a better thermally conductive metal than copper, which is better than stainless steel.

Bowls can be one of two designs. One, like the one Antoine's uses, comes as part of a set with a stand, with an attached plate at the bottom. Notice that Mephistopheles makes an appearance as the stand's legs. Others are shaped more like an oversized Revere bowl that comes with a plate to act as a base on the table. Adler's, a jewelry store in New Orleans, sells this style.

Ladles—derived from the Old English word *hladan*, meaning "to load"—are another important component of making the drink. The ladle that is best for Café Brûlot

The brûlot bowl and cup and saucer used at Antoine's. *Photo by author.*

has its cup angled on both ends, at least one side with a strainer to make sure the cloves, cinnamon, or any other nonliquid ingredients don't get into the drink. The handle is usually wood because who wants to burn their hand on a metal handle!

Having a sturdy, oversized serving fork that can securely hold the orange studded with cloves is a must. A barbecue fork was recommended as an alternative.

Now, if you want to go full-on restaurant style, you could also get a gueridon, a rolling cart for tableside food or drink preparation, which is called "gueridon service."

Opposite: When pouring the coffee into the brûlot cup, use the strainer side of the ladle. *Photo by Chris Granger.*

CHAPTER FOUR

Devil May Care

RECIPES FOR CAFÉ BRÛLOT

Any man who eats dessert is not drinking enough.

—ERNEST HEMINGWAY

Café Brûlot has the distinction of being both a dessert and a flaming coffee drink that combine to create a unique flavor. It is often ordered in place of dessert.

Six New Orleans restaurants provided their recipes for the drink, with each varying their version enough to make it their unique blend. Changes in the recipe, such as not using orange liqueur or replacing French roast coffee with coffee with chicory, do make a difference in taste.

But before we get too far ahead of ourselves, a brief safety lesson is in order. According to a National Fire Protection Association study, cooking contributes to 48 percent of all reported home fires, so it is important to minimize the risk as much as possible. It's smart to have a fire extinguisher on hand, just in case.

One recommendation is to look at a video or read an article about how to make Café Brûlot before your first attempt. "King of Cocktails" Dale DeGroff on the Cocktail Kingdom site is a good one, and Tales of the Cocktail Foundation showcases Arnaud's Charles Abbyad in a photo essay with directions on how to make it.

In addition to the Café Brûlot recipes included here, Brennan's supplied one for Orange Brûlot, with a serving cup as a hollowed-out orange. If you look at old menus from Antoine's, it was once offered there, too, and there is a recipe for it in Lafcadio Hearn's *La Cuisine Créole*.

ƎNTOINE'S

CAFÉ BRÛLOT DIABOLIQUE

SERVES 6

8 whole cloves

2 sticks cinnamon

Peel of one lemon

1½ tablespoons sugar

3 ounces brandy

3 cups strong black coffee, hot

1. Put the cloves, cinnamon, lemon peel, sugar, and brandy in a brûlot bowl or fireproof bowl and heat on an open flame. When the brandy is hot—do not boil—ignite with a match.

2. Use a ladle to stir and pour the liquid around in the bowl for 2 minutes.

3. Pour hot coffee into the flaming brandy and then ladle into brûlot or demitasse cups. (A ladle with a strainer on one end will keep the cloves from getting into the drink.)

Adapted from Antoine's Restaurant, since 1840, Cookbook, *by Roy F. Guste Jr.*

ABOUT ANTOINE'S

When the lights are dimmed at Antoine's Restaurant, it usually means Café Brûlot is about to make the room glow.

Antoine's is a blend of innovation and tradition: dishes such as oysters Rockefeller, oysters Foch, Pompano en Papillote, and eggs Sardou were created here and remain favorites on the menu. The Baked Alaska, while not invented here, was popularized by the restaurant, and no special occasion feels the same without it.

And of course, Antoine's perfected Café Brûlot.

The menus have rarely changed through the years, serving food that fifth-generation owner Rick Blount calls "Haute Creole."

The restaurant's roots are said to go back to France, where the restaurant's founder, Antoine Alciatore, was born in 1822, in Toulon. But according to historian and attorney Ned Hemard, Antoine was actually born Angelo in Alessio, Italy, based on the petition from the succession of his estate. The date of his birth is also up to conjecture, with some sources, such as a 1940 article in the *New Or-*

leans States about the restaurant's one hundredth anniversary, claiming that he was born in 1813 in Marseilles, France.

What is agreed upon is that he grew up Marseilles.

He was apprenticed to the owner of Hôtel de Noailles and ended up in the kitchen. The hotel was considered one of the finest in its day, attracting chefs such as Chef Jean-Louis Françoise-Collinet, who taught Alciatore how to make pommes de terre soufflés, better known as soufflé potatoes, a puffed-up "French fry" served with béarnaise sauce, also invented by Françoise-Collinet.

In 1838, Alciatore decided to move to the United States.

In New Orleans, Alciatore worked at the St. Charles Hotel, just a year old at that point, eventually making his way into the Vieux Carré (French Quarter), where, in 1840, he rented a building at 50 St. Louis Street. There he opened a small pension, a boardinghouse, and restaurant. (It is now the 600 block of St. Louis Street.)

Five years later, he sent for Julie Freyss (sometimes spelled Freysz), whom he had either met on the boat to the United States or in New York, and they married. The businesses were a success, particularly the restaurant, and in 1860, they moved into a larger building, the Lacoul residence, at what is now 714 St. Peter Street.

Success and eight children later, in 1868, the Alciatores purchased a piece of property at 713 St. Louis Street from the Miltenberger family to construct a building that could house their family, guests, and the restaurant. It is the same location of the restaurant today.

In 1877, Alciatore was told by his doctor that he was dying of tuberculosis. He wanted to die in Marseilles, and after making arrangements, he went there, passing away three months later.

Mrs. Alciatore took over the restaurant, soon apprenticing her son, Jules, who was eleven years old. At seventeen, he was sent to France to work in restaurants in Strasbourg, Paris, and Marseilles, with a brief stop in London. Upon returning to New Orleans, he became the chef at the Pickwick Club, before taking over Antoine's.

Jules had inventive flair—and lots of it—creating new dishes and expanding the menu's repertoire with dishes and techniques he had learned overseas. He also enlarged the size of the restaurant, purchasing the buildings around it.

Jules passed away in 1934, and for almost forty years, his son, Roy Alciatore, took over. In 1972 William "Billy" Guste and Roy Guste began running the restaurant, followed by Roy Guste Jr. (1975–84), Bernard "Randy" Guste (1985–2004), and Rick Blount (2005 to the present day).

During his tenure, Blount has renovated the restaurant, careful to keep the original ambiance in the multiple dining rooms, some named after New Orleans Carnival krewes, including Rex, Proteus, and Twelfth Night Revelers. The Hermes Bar, part of the restaurant, is named after that krewe.

Stirring the potent Café Brûlot mixture at Arnaud's. *Photo by Josh Brasted.*

Arnaud's

CAFÉ BRÛLOT

SERVES 6

24 cloves, whole

2 cinnamon sticks

1 lemon

1 orange

4 ounces Grand
Marnier, plus 1
tablespoon

2 ounces brandy, plus
1 tablespoon

32 ounces coffee and
chicory

2 tablespoons sugar,
granulated (you can
adjust sugar to your
taste)

1. Place 12 cloves, cinnamon sticks, and lemon rind in a brûlot bowl.

2. Using a paring knife, peel the orange in a continuous strip, leaving the peel attached to the orange at one end. Stud the orange with 12 cloves, re-coil the peel around it, and place it in the brûlot bowl. Add the Grand Marnier and brandy.

3. Set the brûlot bowl over a flame and allow all the ingredients to heat. Then press a fork into the pulp of the orange, lift it from the bowl, and set it aside momentarily. Pour 1 tablespoon each of Grand Marnier and

brandy into the brûlot bowl and ignite carefully with a long-stemmed match. With your free hand, pick up the orange on the fork and twirl it so the peel twists down into the liquid in the bowl.

4. Pour the flaming alcohol from the ladle down the peel (lights in the room should be dimmed for this), then twice scoop the ladle down into the bowl to get more of the flaming mixture and pour it down around the peel. When the fire burns out, pour the coffee and chicory into the bowl. Add sugar to taste. Discard the orange.

5. Serve in brûlot cups or demitasses.

ABOUT ARNAUD'S

If there is a restaurant that embodies the historical spirit of New Orleans, it is Arnaud's. Opened in 1918, the restaurant can tell a tale of self-proclaimed royalty, jewelry heists, Prohibition arrests, Carnival obsession, and a comeback, all anchored by the restaurant's famed Creole cuisine.

The story starts in Bosdarros, France, on June 27, 1876, when Leon Bertrand Arnaud Cazenave was born. The town is near Pau, in southwestern France, where there is a tradition—including a flaming drink, called Brûlot—that celebrates the harvest of the grapes used to make Armagnac, a brandy.

But first he needed to get to the United States.

After pursuing a career in medicine, Cazenave dreamed of a more glamorous life. Paris, where he went to school, was the obvious choice, but because he wasn't from Paris, it was harder to get a good position there. At age twenty-four, he accepted an invitation from relatives to go to the United States, originally thinking he would practice medicine.

It was not meant to be.

Cazenave became a champagne salesman, and in 1902, he went to New Orleans on a selling trip.

Like many before and after him, he became enchanted with the city's European flair, entrepreneurial spirit, and devil-may-care attitude. And an ambition to own his restaurant began to percolate (if it hadn't already).

He found work in Creole restaurants like La Louisiane and at the Bush and Grunewald Hotels. Almost a decade later, he leased the Old Absinthe House on Bourbon Street, opening a café. Through charm, sartorial splendor, and a knack for entertaining—no doubt the French accent helped—he started being called "Count Arnaud," or just "the Count."

In 1918, the Count heard about an old warehouse on Bienville Street, purchased it, and opened Arnaud's Restaurant. His first chef was a woman, Madame Pierre, with whom he worked to create the menu. Through the years, the Count developed filet de truite Vendôme, suprême de volaille en papillote, oysters Bienville, and filet mignon Clemenceau.

Café Brûlot became a star during the 1920s and 1930s, when a waiter at Arnaud's took the presentation to a theatrical level, according to John DeMers, in *Arnaud's Creole Cookbook: Memoirs and Recipes from the Historic New Orleans Restaurant:*

> A veteran of the French Foreign Legion who had labored in
> no small number of horrid locales, Cézar came up with the
> little tune reminiscent of Offenbach's 'La Belle Hélène' and

tacked on a hodgepodge of words that didn't quite translate in any known language. This serenade, with a host of histrionic gestures, made Cézar's ladling of the flaming Brûlot a ceremony few could forget:

En revenant du sans vree mon
Jubilant! Jubilant!
Pain pain pi na go
La cabinetre
En revenant du sans vree mon
On on on on on!

The really interesting part of this story is that most of Cézar's Café Brûlot performances took place during Prohibition, which lasted from 1920 to 1933. And it was during that time that the Count got in trouble, with fines in 1921 and 1926 and a raid on his home on Esplanade Avenue in 1927. Finally, in 1931, the government launched a sting operation on the restaurant—two agents went in for dinner and were served alcohol—and the Count and two of his waiters were arrested and put in prison. They were indicted for twenty-seven different Prohibition charges, but when the case came up for trial, the Count was acquitted. (No word on the waiters, but I suspect they were too.) Since founding the restaurant, the Count had been purchasing the buildings around him, creating and connecting the multilevel, mazelike structure of thirteen buildings that guests to the restaurant dine in today. Some of the old buildings had previously housed alleged opium dens and houses of prostitution.

The Count passed away in 1948, initially leaving the restaurant to his wife, Lady Irma Cazenave—she got a title too—but his daughter, Germaine Cazenave Wells, who mirrored her father's love of the theatrical and the restaurant worlds, took it over.

She also adored jewels and Carnival, but one treated her better than the other: Wells was robbed several times of her jewels, and she was a queen of more than twenty-two Carnival balls. Her dresses and other memorabilia are now in a small museum in the restaurant. Wells also created an Easter parade, with women bedecked in their finest hats, which still happens in the French Quarter. She passed away in 1983, buried in her favorite Carnival gown—it was the gold lamé she had worn as Queen of Naiads.

Before she passed away, Wells leased the restaurant in 1978, ultimately selling it a few years later, to Archie Casbarian, who, like her father, sought a career and fortune in the United States. They had the same initials, which appealed to Wells too.

Casbarian, who was from Alexandria, Egypt, attended the prestigious HotellerieSuisse of the Société Suisse des Hôteliers in Lausanne, Switzerland, followed by Cornell University's School of Hotel Administration in Ithaca, New York. Casbarian worked in deluxe hotels in Cairo, Washington, DC, and New York, landing in New Orleans at the Royal Sonesta Hotel, where he became general manager. The hotel was across the street from Arnaud's, allowing him to observe the faded beauty and see the potential.

As soon as he took the business leap, Casbarian renovated the buildings and reinvigorated the menu. Café Brûlot was on the menu prepared by Chef Andre Mena for the inaugural dinner on February 28, 1979. Casbarian's wife, Jane, a native of New Orleans, helped him and still works at the restaurant, with their children, Katy Casbarian and Archie Casbarian, who have placed their own mark on the restaurant and the popular French 75 Bar adjacent to it.

BRENNAN'S RESTAURANT

CAFÉ BRÛLOT

SERVES 10 TO 12

1 cinnamon stick,
   4 inches long

10 whole cloves

Peel of 2 oranges,
   cut in thin slices

Peel of 2 lemons,
   cut in thin slices

6 sugar lumps

8 ounces brandy

2 ounces curaçao

1 quart strong black
   coffee

In a brûlot bowl or chafing dish, mash cinnamon, cloves, orange peel, lemon peel, and sugar lumps with ladle. Stir in brandy and curaçao. Carefully ignite brandy and curaçao and mix until sugar lumps are dissolved. Gradually add brewed black coffee and continue mixing until flame flickers out. Serve hot in brûlot or demitasse cups.

Note: If you can, use a ladle with one side having a strainer so bits of the cinnamon, cloves, and fruit peels don't go into the drink when it is being poured into a cup.

ORANGE BRÛLOT

SERVES 1

1 thin-skin orange, washed and dried
1½ ounces cognac
2 sugar lumps

1. *Orange prep:* Plunge orange into hot water for five minutes. Then, with a sharp pointed knife, cut through the peel only of the orange's center. Insert the edge of a spoon between the skin and pull, working around the fruit of the orange, separating the two. Carefully roll the skin up from the pulp, turning it inside out–the upper half as the cup, the lower half as the stand for the orange. Then re-form so the skin side is outside.

2. *The drink:* Fill the upper half, the cup, with cognac. Put lumps of sugar in a teaspoon filled with cognac and ignite. When the sugar begins to color, gently float it onto the surface of the cognac in the orange cup. When the flame flickers, blow it out.

ABOUT BRENNAN'S RESTAURANT

It was the 1940s, and Owen Brennan was the proprietor of the Old Absinthe House, a bar in the French Quarter. One of his customers was Count Arnaud Cazenave of Arnaud's. The Count, who was from France, prided himself on his culinary worldliness, or let's just say his je ne sais quoi. He would stop in to tease Brennan that he didn't think "an Irishman," as he was quoted as saying, could run a decent restaurant with good food.

Game on.

Brennan's great-great-grandfather, the first Owen Brennan, had arrived from Ireland in the 1840s, fleeing the potato famine that had decimated the country and caused mass emigration.

He settled in New Orleans, where he had a son, also named Owen, who had a son named Owen (Owen Patrick Brennan).

Owen Patrick met Ella "Nell" Valentine at a dance, and the two were soon married. Owen rose through the ranks to become the supervisor of shipbuilding at Johnson

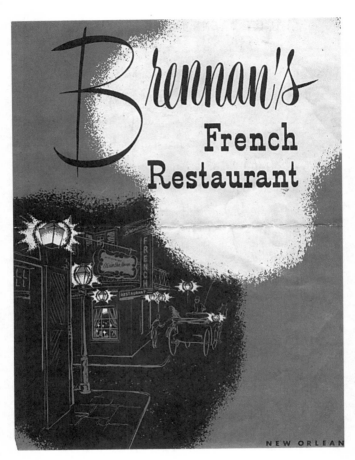

Vintage menu from Brennan's. *Photo courtesy of Brennan's Restaurant.*

Iron Works, and Nell took care of the home. They had six children: Owen Edward, Adelaide, John, Ella, Dick, and Dottie.

Owen Edward Brennan had acquired the Old Absinthe House as a business in which he and his siblings could all participate and as a way to support their parents as they got older. Before that, he had bought a gas station and drugstore near City Park and, during World War II, helped the owner of the Court of Two Sisters, who was serving in the war, run that restaurant.

In 1946, Brennan purchased the Vieux Carré Restaurant on Bourbon Street, directly across the street from the bar. The restaurant was down on its heels, but Brennan and his siblings transformed it into a successful business, so much so that they started looking for a bigger property. They also had a more practical reason: the lease for the building was about to end in May 1956. Brennan started looking and found what he wanted at 417 Royal Street.

Unfortunately, Brennan did not live to see the new restaurant open, passing away six months before then, in

1955. His family still launched the restaurant and continued to run it. It wasn't until 1973 that Brennan's widow, Maude, wanted to run the restaurant with her children, Pip (Owen Edward Jr.), who was already working there, Jimmy, and Ted. Brennan's siblings left, getting, in the division of the assets, the Friendship House in Biloxi, Mississippi (no longer open) and Commander's Palace, which they had purchased in 1969.

The Brennan's Restaurant traditions continued, including the famous "Breakfast at Brennan's" and the menu of French-Creole cuisine, along with original dishes such as bananas Foster and eggs Hussarde.

The restaurant was also known for its distinctive pink building, built in 1795 by the great-grandfather of French artist Edgar Degas. It subsequently housed the Louisiana State Bank and was a private residence to chess master Paul Morphy, for whom there is a room named after him in the current restaurant. After being bequeathed to Tulane University, the Brennan family leased the building in 1954, then bought it in 1984.

In 2013, Terry White and Ralph Brennan, nephew to Owen Brennan, purchased the restaurant and undertook a major physical and culinary renovation, with glamorous new interiors by Richard Keith Langham and a new take on cuisine that reinvigorated the menu while keeping some favorite dishes.

CAFÉ BRÛLOT

SERVES 4 TO 6

Café Brûlot mix:

8 ounces cognac

4 ounces brandy

8 to 10 whole cloves

2 whole cinnamon
  sticks

One orange peel,
  4 to 6 inches long

One lemon peel,
  3 to 4 inches long

Mix the ingredients and allow to infuse overnight in the refrigerator for 24 to 36 hours. After that, strain out the cloves, cinnamon stick, and peels. Will keep for 2 to 3 weeks.

When making the Café Brûlot:

8 to 10 cloves

Demerara syrup (equal parts sugar to water)

4 to 6 cups strong coffee (preferably dark French roast)

1. Prepare a long, wide orange zest spiral studded with 8 to 10 cloves. Puncture the orange with a serving fork and set it aside.

2. Heat a copper bowl over an open flame. Pour Café Brûlot mixture into the copper bowl. When the mixture warms up, ladle a small amount and expose it to the open flame below the bowl, using it to ignite the rest of the mixture in the bowl.

3. Pick up the fork with the studded orange and position it over the center of the bowl with the spiral dangling into the mixture. Using the ladle, slowly pour the flaming mixture over the peel. The oil in the peel will provide a nice light show. Do this several times, then pour the coffee slowly into the bowl until the fire is extinguished.

4. Sweeten the mixture to taste with the warmed demerara sugar syrup. Serve in demitasse or coffee cups.

ABOUT BROUSSARD'S

When Broussard's Restaurant opened in 1920, it was the culmination of a dream for chef and raconteur Joseph Cezaire Broussard. Born in 1891 in Loreauville, Louisiana, Broussard moved to New Orleans in 1902, eventually working in a number of restaurants, including Antoine's, where he was employed by Jules Alciatore as a waiter and in the kitchen. He attended culinary school in Paris from 1910 to 1914 and was a chef's assistant to Chef Mornay Voiron at Restaurant Durand.

After marrying Rosalie Borrello Broussard and working in several restaurants, the couple opened Broussard's in Rosalie's childhood home. Her parents, Mary Ann and Antoine Borrello, had given the building to the newlyweds as a wedding gift. (The couple lived above the restaurant for forty years.)

The restaurant menu was a blend of the city's Creole and French cuisine, with some influences from Rosalie's Italian heritage and Joseph's French training.

Broussard once said, "Never trust a lean cook," and in a 1952 article in the *New Orleans Item* newspaper, Broussard claimed he had invented up to eighty-five dishes, including chicken papillote (chicken baked with fresh mushrooms in an oiled paper bag), crêpes Suzette soufflé, and a variety of dishes "à la Broussard."

"I was forced to call them 'à la Broussard' because I always add something to the original recipes," Broussard had said in an earlier *New Orleans Item* article from 1926.

A fan of Napoleon brandy, Broussard would have his waiters salute the statue of Napoleon Bonaparte and ring a bell in the restaurant's courtyard when an order was placed for the drink. The tradition stopped in 1966, when Broussard passed away, a little more than a month after the death of his wife, Rosalie.

Their descendants ran the restaurant for a while, before it was purchased in 1974 by Joseph Segreto, with Joseph C. Marcello and Joseph Marcello Jr. as partners. In 1984, Evelyn and Chef Gunter Preuss became part owners, and by 1993, they had taken over as sole owners of the restaurant.

Broussard's consists of multiple buildings of different periods and ownership that were eventually linked together in the early twentieth century by the restaurant's founder.

The Magnolia Room, which is currently used as a dining room, is the oldest building on the property. It was originally built as a separate stable for Samuel Hermann, whose house was designed by architect William Brand in

1831. (Now called Hermann-Grima House, it is a historic house museum, located behind the restaurant's courtyard fence, facing St. Louis Street.)

In 1844, Felix Grima and his family moved into the home, and in 1896, Grima fell into financial hardship, selling the property on which the restaurant sits.

Broussard's Josephine Room was built in 1876 and was used as the washroom for the home. A small Creole cottage once occupied the area fronting Conti Street. From 1835 to 1885, that building housed the Jefferson Academy, a boys' school that went from primary grade to "completion of the academic course in a curriculum of English, French, writing, mathematics, geography, history, bookkeeping and fencing," according to the *Broussard's Restaurant Cookbook*, published in 1996.

Many alterations were made over the years, and in 1974, Samuel Wilson Jr. of Koch and Wilson Architects, designer Charles Gresham, and artist Charles Reinike oversaw an extensive, twenty-six-month-long remodeling of the buildings.

In 2013, when Creole Cuisine Restaurant Concepts—owned by brothers Marv, Richy, and Zeid Ammari—bought the business, the property was in need of another renovation, including updates to electrical and mechanical systems. Brian Bockman and Jack Forbes of Bockman Forbes Design were brought in as architects, and Constance Restoration oversaw the more than one-million-dollar remodel. The changes included the entry hall's walls, which were brought back to the Venetian finish from the early days of the restaurant.

The menu still features longtime favorites such as oysters Broussard and its variation on oysters Rockefeller, and other signature dishes include pompano Pontchartrain.

COMMANDER'S PALACE

CAFÉ BRÛLOT

SERVES 2

1 lemon

1 orange

2 dozen whole cloves

1½ ounces triple sec

1 ounce brandy

2 cinnamon sticks

1½ cups strong black coffee

1. Peel the lemon, in one continuous motion so that the peel is in a long spiral, over a heatproof bowl in order to catch the juices. Discard the pulp or reserve for another use. Repeat with the orange. Insert the cloves into both peels at 1-inch intervals. Spear both peels at one end with the tines of a large fork and set aside.

2. Heat the triple sec, brandy, and cinnamon sticks in a saucepan. When hot, carefully ignite the mixture with a long-handled match. Holding the fork with the citrus peels, ladle the flaming brandy down the peels.

3. Gradually add the coffee, pouring it around the edges of the saucepan to extinguish the flames. Ladle the coffee into 2 heatproof coffee cups or Irish coffee mugs and serve immediately. (The restaurant uses

Sterno for a heat source. They recommend using a 2½-quart saucepan when preparing the drink at home.]

From In the Land of Cocktails: Recipes and Adventures
from the Cocktail Chicks, *by Ti Adelaide Martin and Lally Brennan*

ABOUT COMMANDER'S PALACE

It's hard to miss the turquoise blue Victorian building on the corner of Washington Avenue and Coliseum Street in New Orleans.

This beacon of culinary excellence is the location of Commander's Palace—painted in what is called "Commander's Blue"—and the restaurant is much more than a jaunty color.

The restaurant was not only an incubator for tradition-meets-innovative cuisine with roots in Louisiana; it also launched the careers of chefs Paul Prudhomme, Emeril Lagasse, Jamie Shannon, Tory McPhail, and Meg Bickford.

Nice work for what started as a saloon in 1893. It was Emile Commander, the restaurant's namesake, who segued the saloon into a restaurant, making it the toast of the town. In the 1920s, Frank G. Giarratano purchased the restaurant, followed by Elinor and Frank Moran, who took over in 1944.

The Brennan family purchased the restaurant in 1969, and in 1973, siblings Ella, Adelaide, John, Dick, and Dottie took it over when they left Brennan's Restaurant.

Ella Brennan was the exacting taskmaster of the restaurant, providing chefs with the space for creating imaginative dishes and pushing culinary boundaries. Longtime favorite dishes at the restaurant include turtle soup, shrimp and tasso Henican, spiced sugarcane lacquered quail, and bread pudding soufflé.

Today the restaurant is managed by Ella Brennan's daughter, Ti Adelaide Martin, and John Brennan's daughter, Lally Brennan.

Galatoire's

CAFÉ BRÛLOT

SERVES 6

1 orange

1 lemon

12 whole cloves

3 cinnamon sticks

2 ounces brandy

2 ounces orange liqueur, such as curaçao

2 tablespoons sugar

6 cups brewed French roast coffee, kept hot

1. Carefully carve a continuous peel from an orange. Cut the lemon peel into quarter-inch curls and set aside. (See note following recipe.) Stud the orange peel with the cloves and spear one end of the coil with a fork. Keep the clove-studded flesh of the orange and lemon for some other use.

2. In a small saucepan, combine lemon peel, cinnamon sticks, brandy, orange liqueur, and sugar over low heat until very warm, to allow the ingredients to marry. The warmth is also required to ignite the Café Brûlot; cold liquor will not flame. Once the ingredients are heated, pour them into a brûlot bowl or a stainless steel bowl that has a flat bottom. Ignite the liquor by holding

a match to a ladle full of the liquor. Once the ladle is lit, slowly lower it to the liquor in the bowl.

3. Hold the fork with the dangling clove-studded orange coil over the ignited bowl. Take extreme care not to burn yourself. Stir the flaming liquor with the ladle and spoon the liquor over the orange coil you are holding over the bowl. The flame will spiral down the coil of orange peel and cloves, back into the bowl. Once you have poured the flaming liquor down the coil several times to incorporate the flavors, remove the coil from the fork and put it in the bowl.

4. Slowly pour in the coffee while stirring, to extinguish the flame.

5. Ladle small amounts of the aromatic mixture into demitasse cups.

Note: While it may not make a striking presentation, an option for the home cook is to simply cut the peel from the citrus fruits and remove the pith, instead of curling the peel into elaborate coils. The pieces of orange can then be studded with the cloves.

Adapted from Galatoire's Cookbook: Recipes and Family History from the Time-Honored New Orleans Restaurant, *by Melvin Rodrigue and Jyl Benson*

Opposite: Café Brûlot being made at Galatoire's. *Photo courtesy of Galatoire's Restaurant.*

ABOUT GALATOIRE'S

When Jean Galatoire left his small town of Pardies, located in the foothills of the Pyrenees Mountains, near Pau, France, little did he know he was making the first steps toward creating the Galatoire's mystique.

Anyone who has dined here knows about this mystique: the legendary "Friday at Galatoire's," where lunch is always a party; the no-reservation policy for the main dining room and lines to get into the restaurant; the furor over crushed ice versus cubed ice in 1994; the house accounts; having your own waiter; and of course, the food that doesn't waver in its French roots.

Playwright Tennessee Williams found the restaurant so alluring that he had a regular table and mentioned Galatoire's in *A Streetcar Named Desire.*

Galatoire departed France in 1874, first settling with his wife, Gabrielle Marchal Galatoire, in Birmingham, Alabama, where he bought an inn and restaurant. After a brief stint in Chicago, they arrived in New Orleans around 1900.

Galatoire opened a bar near the Louisville & Nashville (L&N) train station, at the foot of Canal Street. He brought over his nephew Justin Galatoire in 1902 to help with the business. Galatoire soon sold the bar to purchase Victor's, a restaurant established in the mid-1800s. He changed the name to Galatoire's and opened the doors at 209 Bourbon Street in 1905. The new restaurant featured a mix of traditional French recipes combined with some from the Victor's menu. Galatoire owned the business but not the building, which he was able to buy in 1911.

Justin Galatoire's brother Leon immigrated to the United States in 1906, followed by Gabriel in 1912. Seven years later, Jean Galatoire sold the business to his three nephews. His health failing, he died later that year, at age sixty-five.

The restaurant remained in the family for years, maintaining its high standards for food and known as a place where frivolity ruled.

It wasn't until 1999 that there was a major renovation done to the building, with the second floor (which had been closed during World War II) reopened for additional dining and a bar for waiting customers. In April 2013, Galatoire's "33," a bar and steakhouse, was opened next door. Louisiana businessman John Georges is the majority owner of both restaurants, which are also owned and partly operated by several descendants of the Galatoire family.

CHAPTER FIVE

Devil in Disguise

FLAMING DRINKS AND DESSERTS—
BEYOND CAFÉ BRÛLOT

One cannot think well, love well, sleep well, if one has not dined well.

—VIRGINIA WOOLF, *A Room of One's Own*

As much as Café Brûlot is a showstopping spectacle, it does have some fiery cousins joining it in the culinary and libationary realms.

What is the allure of flaming drinks and desserts? The danger and the "wow" factor are obvious to the spectator, but a more practical aspect is that the heat often enhances the flavors.

They key to lighting drinks or food on fire is the alcohol needs to be 80 proof or above; the higher the proof, the easier it is to ignite.

And before you make anything that you have to light on fire, always make sure you have a fire extinguisher ready to go.

Let's ignite this chapter and read on!

DRINKS

Like Café Brûlot, most of these drinks have more than one origin story, but all end up with the same result—a great cocktail.

Even though the first recipe for a flaming drink wasn't put into a book until 1862, it would be safe to assume that flaming drinks had been entertaining people before that time.

That book, *Bon Vivant's Companion,* by Jerry Thomas, includes a recipe for the **Blue Blazer,** an intoxicating brew of high-proof Scotch whiskey, boiling water, and white sugar finished with a lemon peel. It's much like a hot toddy, minus the cinnamon stick, lemon juice, and honey (in place of the Blue Blazer's sugar). The entertaining part comes when the bartender pours the drink back and forth between two solid metal cups, with the fire streaming between.

Anyone who has gone to college in the United States has probably sampled a **Flaming Dr. Pepper Shot.** It starts with a shot glass, in which amaretto is topped with 151 proof rum, then lit on fire, and dropped into a mug of beer. Chugging ensues, with drinkers swearing that it tastes just like Dr. Pepper soda.

There are two claims for who invented the shot: Luke Cemino at the Ptarmigan Club in Bryan, Texas, or Dave Brinks at the Gold Mine Saloon in New Orleans.

The Ptarmigan Club, a former bordello, was popular with the nearby Texas A&M University crowd. It was also not far—about eighty-eight miles—from Waco, Texas, where Dr. Pepper was invented by a pharmacist, Charles Alderton, around 1885.

Luke Cemino, who purchased the club in 1976, was said to have invented the shot sometime afterward, then it was spread far and wide by Texas A&M students and those who visited the bar.

That said, in 1986, Dave Brinks was helping his mother out at her New Orleans bar, the Gold Mine Saloon, and decided to do a "shot" menu, with one of them tasting like his favorite drink, the Dr. Pepper. It was a hit.

Another shot is the **B-52**, layered with coffee liqueur, Irish Cream, Grand Marnier, and sometimes a dash of rum. (As with most cocktails, there are variations.) The shot can be sampled as is or lit on fire. If you use the flaming option, recipes say to insert a straw and drink very, very quickly.

The origins of the B-52 are not well documented, so there are a few origin claims: it was invented by Peter Fich, a head bartender at the Banff Springs Hotel in Alberta, in 1977, naming it after his favorite band, the B-52s; or by

Adam Honigman, a bartender at Maxwell's Plum in New York City.

A tropical drink with a voodoo imprimatur, the **Zombie** was concocted in 1934 by Donn Beach at his Don the Beachcomber restaurant in Hollywood, California. Allegedly, it was for a hungover customer, who returned days later to say that he had been turned into a "zombie." The ingredients include three types of rum, lime juice, Falernum, Angostura bitters, Pernod, grenadine, and "Donn's juice," consisting of cinnamon syrup and grapefruit juice, all mixed together and served in a tiki glass. The original recipe was not set on fire.

Because Donn kept the recipe a closely guarded secret, there have been variations of it, some with and without the flame, which was no doubt the inspiration for the presentation of other fiery tiki-style cocktails, such as the Scorpion and Flaming Volcano.

Jeff "Beachbum" Berry, a tropical drink enthusiast and owner of Latitude 29 in New Orleans, said he tracked down the original recipe and has it on his website.

FOOD

It's no surprise that many flaming desserts can be found on the menus of a number of old-line New Orleans restaurants.

A flamboyant end to a meal at Brennan's Restaurant is **Bananas Foster,** a sumptuous blend of bananas, butter, brown sugar, cinnamon, banana liqueur, and rum, which are lit on fire and, after the alcohol burns out, served over vanilla ice cream.

There are two stories on how the dessert was invented, converging at the year it was created, 1951, and who the dessert was named after: Richard Foster, the chairman of the New Orleans Crime Commission.

One version says Owen Brennan challenged his chef Paul Blangé at Brennan's to create a dish featuring the fruit that had arrived in the kitchen courtesy of Owen's brother John, who ran a produce business.

The other is from *Miss Ella of Commander's Palace,* the memoir by the late restaurateur Ella Brennan, Owen's sister. Ella was managing Vieux Carré Restaurant, the predecessor of Brennan's, when Owen tasked her to come up with a special new dessert for a dinner in honor of Richard Foster.

Ella recalled a dish of caramelized bananas that her mother, Nellie, would make for breakfast. Using that dish as the spark for a new dish, she grabbed the bananas, sautéing them with butter and brown sugar. The restaurant's maître d', Frank Bertucci, reminded her about the pizzazz of Antoine's Baked Alaska, another flaming dessert, so Ella added rum and banana liqueur to the mixture, lit it on fire, and, after the flame went out, served it over vanilla ice cream.

Speaking of that **Baked Alaska,** while it wasn't invented in New Orleans, it was perfected there, at Antoine's, where the dessert is a favorite for celebratory events.

The genesis of this dessert was with American-born physicist and inventor Sir Benjamin Thompson, Count Rumford, who was living in Europe at the turn of the nineteenth century.

His inventions include the double boiler, the sous vide cooking method, thermal underwear, a kitchen range, and

Baked Alaska at Antoine's. *Photo courtesy of Antoine's Restaurant.*

a drip coffeepot. Another discovery? That whipped egg whites in a meringue made an excellent insulator.

By the 1830s, French chefs were using his discovery to create a dish called the "omelette Norwegge" (also called "omelette Norvégienne"), consisting of layers of cake and ice cream covered in meringue, then broiled. Antoine Alciatore most likely encountered it while he was training at the Hôtel de Noailles in Marseilles.

But there is another claim to the creation of the American version of Baked Alaska: Charles Ranhofer, the Parisian expat chef at Delmonico's in New York City. (Delmonico's was established in 1837.) Ranhofer, who trained as a chef in Europe, most likely encountered the omelette Norwegge. He also liked to give new dishes names that had a cultural relevancy, such as Peach Pudding à la [President Grover] Cleveland or Sarah Potatoes, after Sarah Bernhardt.

So, it's not surprising that Ranhofer combined two historic events—the United States' purchase of Alaska from Russia in 1867 and Florida becoming a state in 1845—to name his dessert the "Alaska, Florida," creatively representing the cold-hot elements of the recipe.

The Alaska, Florida recipe appeared in Ranhofer's 1894 cookbook, *The Epicurean*. The main difference with the omelette Norwegge and Ranhofer's version against Antoine's Restaurant's version is that while the first two are broiled to give the meringue a toasted look, the concoction made at Antoine's is presented on fire via brandy, which some culinarians also call a "bombe Alaska." Confusing matters further is that the dish appeared on the Antoine's menu as "omelette Historiée à la Jules Cesar" and, on later menus, as "omelette Alaska Antoine."

The alternative version comes from Michael Krondl, associate editor of the *Oxford Companion to Sugar and Sweets*: Krondl theorizes the French omelette Norwegge didn't appear until the 1890s, and the evidence for Ranhofer's Alaska, Florida isn't enough to credit him with the creation of the dessert.

In addition to bananas Foster and Café Brûlot, **Crêpes Suzette** is a tableside treat with the gueridon presentation—from start to finish—always one of the high points of a meal. This dessert consists of crepes made with "beurre Suzette" (a sauce of sugar, butter, orange juice, and Grand Marnier or another orange liqueur) ladled on top, then lit on fire.

As to be expected, there are a different claims to the origin of the dish. In 1895, at Café de Paris in Monte Carlo, a fourteen-year-old assistant waiter named Henri Charpentier made the dessert for the Prince of Wales, who in six years would be King Edward VII of the United Kingdom.

One of the guests at the table was a Frenchwoman named Suzette. However, in an interview in the 1950s, Charpentier said it was based on a recipe his mother had made, the liqueur added to the dish because it was the thing to do then.

Yet another story alleges the dish was named in honor of French actress Suzanne Reichenberg, who was known professionally as Suzette. While onstage, she was portraying a maid and served crêpes as part of the role. The owner of Restaurant Marivaux provided the crêpes, which he flambéed to wow the audience and keep the food warm for the actors and actresses.

And probably the simplest of the flaming desserts to prepare: **Cherries Jubilee.** This dessert is made of cherries and liqueur, usually Kirschwasser, then lit on fire and served over vanilla ice cream. The recipe is generally credited to Georges-Auguste Escoffier, who prepared the dish for Queen Victoria, who loved cherries, for her Jubilee celebration in 1887. The original version did not have ice cream.

RESOURCES

BOOKS

Some of these works provided information for this text;
others are just great reads.

Baird, Sarah. *New Orleans Cocktails: An Elegant Collection of Over 100 Recipes Inspired by the Big Easy.* Kennebunkport, ME: Cider Mill Press, 2017.

Bannos, Jimmy, and John DeMers. *Big Easy Cocktails: Jazzy Drinks and Savory Bites from New Orleans.* Berkeley, CA: Ten Speed Press, 2006.

Benoit, Ann, and the Preuss family. *Broussard's Restaurant & Courtyard Cookbook.* New Orleans: Pelican Publishing, 2012.

Berry, Jeff "Beachbum." *Potions of the Caribbean.* New York: Cocktail Kingdom, 2013.

Brennan, Ella, and Ti Adelaide Martin. *Miss Ella of Commander's Palace: I Don't Want a Restaurant Where a Jazz Band Can't Come Marching Through.* Layton, UT: Gibbs Smith, 2016.

Brennan, Pip, Jimmy, and Ted. *Breakfast at Brennan's and Dinner, Too.* New Orleans: Brennan's, 1994.

Burton, Marda, and Kenneth Holditch. *Galatoire's: Biography of a Bistro.* Athens, GA: Hill Street Press, 2004.

Carter, Hodding, ed. *The Past as Prelude: New Orleans, 1718–1968*. New Orleans: Tulane University Publication / Pelican Publishing, 1968.

Christian Woman's Exchange (New Orleans). *The Creole Cookery Book*. 1st ed. 1885. Reprint, Gretna, LA: Pelican Publishing, 2005.

Collier, Phillip, and Jennifer Adams. *Phillip Collier's Mixing New Orleans: Cocktails and Legends*. New Orleans: Philbeau Publishing, 2007.

Curnonsky. *Traditional Recipes of the Provinces of France*. Translated by Edwin Lavin. New York: Doubleday & Co., 1961.

Curtis, Wayne. *And a Bottle of Rum: A History of the New World in Ten Cocktails*. New York: Broadway Books, 2006. Revised and updated 2018.

DeMers, John. *Arnaud's Creole Cookbook: Memoirs and Recipes from the Historic New Orleans Restaurant*. Preface by Archie Casbarian. New York: Simon & Schuster, 1988.

Deutsch, Hermann B. *Brennan's New Orleans Cookbook*. New Orleans: Robert L. Crager & Co., 1964.

Guste, Roy F., Jr. *Antoine's Restaurant, since 1840, Cookbook: A Collection of the Original Recipes from New Orleans' Oldest and Most Famous Restaurant*. 1978. Reprint, New Orleans: Guste Publishing, 2005.

Hearn, Lafcadio. *Lafcadio Hearn's Creole Cookbook*. (Originally published as *La Cuisine Créole* in 1885.) Reprint, New Orleans: Pelican Publishing Co., 1990.

Hémard, Ned. *Ned Hémard's Nostalgia*. New Orleans Bar Association website. https://www.neworleansbar.org/new-orleans-nostalgia. (This collection of articles by Hémard is a huge source of historical information about New Orleans.)

Jones, Caroline Merrick. *Gourmet's Guide to New Orleans: Creole Cookbook*. 18th ed. 1933. Reprint, New Orleans: Caroline Merrick Jones, 1965.

Keyes, Frances Parkinson. *Dinner at Antoine's*. New York: Julian Messner,

1948. (The book opens with a party at Antoine's that ends in mystery and murder.)

Louisiana Almanac. New Orleans: Pelican Publishing, 1968–.

Martin, Ti Adelaide, and Lally Brennan. *In the Land of Cocktails: Recipes and Adventures from the Cocktail Chicks.* New York: William Morrow Cookbooks, 2007.

Martin, Ti Adelaide, and Jamie Shannon. *Commander's Kitchen: Take Home the True Tastes of New Orleans with More than 150 Recipes from Commander's Palace Restaurant.* Portland, OR: Broadway Books, 2000.

McCaffety, Kerry. *Etouffée, Mon Amour: The Great Restaurants of New Orleans.* New Orleans: Pelican Publishing, 2002.

———. *Obituary Cocktail: The Great Saloons of New Orleans.* New Orleans: Pelican Publishing, 1998.

Preuss, Gunther, and Evelyn Preuss. *Broussard's Restaurant Cookbook.* New Orleans: Pelican Publishing, 1996.

Rodrigue, Melvin, with Jyl Benson. *Galatoire's Cookbook: Recipes and Family History from the Time-Honored New Orleans Restaurant.* New York: Clarkson N. Potter, 2005.

Tooker, Poppy. *Louisiana Eats! The People, the Food, and Their Stories.* New Orleans: Pelican Publishing, 2013.

Tucker, Susan, and S. Frederick Starr. *New Orleans Cuisine: Louisiana's Signature Dishes and Their Histories.* Jackson: University Press of Mississippi, 2009.

Wells, Germaine Cazenave. *The Story of Arnaud's.* New Orleans: Arnaud's, 1950. (Available at Tulane University's digital archives: https://digital library.tulane.edu/islandora/object/tulane%3A18399/datastream /PDF/view.)

Williams, Elizabeth M., and Chris McMillian. *Lift Your Spirits: A Celebratory*

History of Cocktail Culture in New Orleans. The Southern Table. Baton Rouge: Louisiana State University Press, 2016.

Wohl, Kit. *Arnaud's Restaurant Cookbook: New Orleans Legendary Creole Cuisine.* New Orleans: Pelican Publishing, 2005.

————. *New Orleans Classic Cocktails.* New Orleans: Pelican Publishing, 2012.

Wolfert, Paula. *The Cooking of Southwest France: Recipes from France's Magnificent Rustic Cuisine.* 1st ed. 1983. Reprint, Hoboken, NJ: John Wiley & Sons, 2005.

Wondrich, David. *Imbibe! From Absinthe to Whiskey Smash, a Salute in Stories and Drinks to "Professor" Jerry Thomas, Pioneer of the American Bar.* Updated and revised. New York: TarcherPerigee, 2015.

VISUALS

Brasted, Josh. "How to Make the Famous Café Brûlot from Arnaud's," March 22, 2017, Tales of the Cocktail Foundation website, https://talesofthecocktail.org/techniques/how-make-arnauds-cafe-brulot/.

Cocktail Kingdom. "The History of the Café Brûlot with Dale DeGroff," pts. 1–3, available on YouTube. Video.

CULINARY HISTORY

Historic New Orleans Collection | 520 and 533 Royal St., New Orleans 504.523.4662 | hnoc.org (This site is a great resource, along with the collection's Williams Resource Center.)

John and Bonnie Boyd Hospitality and Culinary Library (part of the
    Southern Food & Beverage Museum) | 1840 Euterpe St.,
    New Orleans | 504.569.0405 (by appointment) | southernfood.org
New Orleans Public Library | Nolalibrary.org
Restaurant Collection, Louisiana Research Collection, Tulane University
    Special Collections, Howard-Tilton Memorial Library, New Orleans
    www.library.tulane.edu
Southern Food & Beverage Museum/The Museum of the American
    Cocktail | 1504 Oretha Castle Haley Blvd., New Orleans
    504.569.0405 | southernfood.org

PLACES TO SAMPLE CAFÉ BRÛLOT

Antoine's Restaurant | 713 St. Louis St., New Orleans | 504.581.4422
    antoines.com
Arnaud's Restaurant | 813 Bienville St., New Orleans | 504.523.5433
    arnaudsrestaurant.com
Brennan's Restaurant | 417 Royal St., New Orleans | 504.525.9711
    brennansneworleans.com
Broussard's | 819 Conti St., New Orleans | 504.581.3866 | broussards.com
Commander's Palace | 1403 Washington Ave., New Orleans
    504.899.8221 | commanderspalace.com
Galatoire's Restaurant | 209 Bourbon St., New Orleans | 504.525.2021
    galatoires.com

PLACES TO PURCHASE CAFÉ BRÛLOT
UTENSILS AND ACCESSORIES

NEW

Adler's | Various locations | Adlersjewelry.com
Cocktail Kingdom | Cocktailkingdom.com

ANTIQUE

Decorations Lucullus | 915 Kentucky St., New Orleans | 504.528.9620
    decorationslucullus.com
eBay
Keil's Antiques | 325 Royal St., New Orleans | 504.522.4552
    keilsantiques.com